Kiwi Health Heroes

By Caitlin Timmer-Arends, Rebecca Waddell & So-Young Cho

Contents

Health Care 40

Health Triumphs 53

Advice from our Health Heroes 69

Welcome to Kiwi Health Heroes!

You're about to embark on a journey through time and discovery, where real-life Kiwi legends have changed the way that we think about and care for our health. From daring doctors and brilliant inventors to everyday heroes who never gave up, these are the stories of people who made a difference — just like you can!

Did you know that a New Zealand inventor created the first ever disposable syringe? Or that a rural doctor made a world-first discovery about chronic fatigue syndrome? How about the amazing Kiwi who started air rescues after witnessing a disaster? And let's not forget the clever minds behind incredible inventions like high-tech medical imaging that's helping save lives today!

But this adventure isn't just about looking back — it's about stepping into the shoes of a health hero yourself. In this book, you'll be able to pick your reading path, leading you from one story to the next. Will you follow the path of brave caregivers? Or explore the minds of inventors who changed health forever? Maybe you'll uncover the stories of Kiwis who faced huge health battles — and won! The choice is yours.

So, are you ready to explore the past, be inspired by the present, and discover how you can be a Kiwi health hero, too? Let's go!

Health History

Aotearoa has amazing health stories from the past! Here you can find stories about the first female army doctor in New Zealand, the man who started air rescues after seeing the *Wahine* disaster, and Nurse Maude, who helped so many people in her community. Then there's the Tapanui GP who discovered chronic fatigue syndrome – a world first! Enjoy reading about these inspiring Kiwis who made a big difference.

1. **Nurse Maude:** The story of Sibylla Maude
2. **Hope Soars:** The story of Peter Button
3. **When Adults Think You're Sick Because You Saw a Cow:** The story of Hannah Butler
4. **Being Brave:** The story of George Hamlin
5. **Being the First:** The story of Jean Sandel
6. **Travelling the World to Help at Home:** The story of Elizabeth Gunn
7. **Snow Bound for Tapanui:** The story of Peter Snow

Nurse Maude

The story of Sibylla Maude

Thomas and Emily Maude lived in Christchurch and had eight children. Their first child was born on 11 August 1862, and they named her Emily Sibylla Maude. Because she had the same first name as her mum, everyone called her Sibylla. Sibylla cared for people her whole life, starting with her seven younger brothers and sisters.

When she grew up, Sibylla went all the way to London to learn how to be a nurse. It was 1889 and planes hadn't been invented yet, so Sibylla had to travel to the other side of the world on a ship. It took two years for her to learn everything she could about nursing, and then she came home to Christchurch to her new job as the matron of Christchurch Hospital.

Working in a hospital wasn't what Sibylla wanted to do for the rest of her life. She was an independent spirit and wanted more freedom to help people than a hospital could give her. She wanted to help sick people in their homes, especially people who couldn't afford to go to hospital — which is now known as district nursing.

Did you know?

In 1902, New Zealand was the first country in the whole world to register nurses! Before the Second World War, if you needed to go to hospital, you had to pay to stay there. That meant lots of people couldn't afford to get help when they were sick.

Sibylla talked to some friends to see if she could get enough support to start visiting sick people at home. She was friends with the Anglican Sisters of the Community of the Sacred Name and was also a member of St Michael and All Angels Church. Sibylla told the vicar, Reverend Walter Averill, what she wanted to do. Reverend Averill talked to Reverend Edwin Scott, the Vicar of St Saviours, and the two churches gave Sibylla their support.

Two of Sibylla's good friends, Heaton and Jessie Rhodes, gave Sibylla money to get started. With their support, and the support of the two churches, district nursing was born. Sibylla began making visits to people's homes on 5 November 1896. Really quickly, Sibylla — or Nurse Maude as everyone knew her — became a household name. More and more people came to her for help. Within a year, she had made over one thousand visits on foot to people who couldn't afford hospital

DISTRICT NURSING OFFICE

or private nursing care. Within five years, there was so much work that the Nurse Maude District Nursing Association was formed. There were now eight district nurses! They all had bicycles, because visiting people on foot was hard work.

Nurse Maude noticed on her rounds that people at home didn't really know how to treat diseases. Tuberculosis (too-ber-kew-LO-sis) was a scary disease, and Sibylla had some ideas on how to help people. She talked to two doctors, Dr Alice Moorhouse and Dr Leslie Crooke, about her ideas. With their support, she started two open-air camps in the New Brighton sand dunes. People at the camps got better – her ideas were working! Lots of people supported Sibylla and donated money for the camps.

Did you know?

Heaton Rhodes, who helped Sibylla by giving her money to start district nursing, became the Minister of Public Health in 1912. During the First World War, he looked into how sick New Zealand soldiers were being treated, and saved many lives. He also worked for the New Zealand branch of the British Red Cross Society. He and Sibylla must have had a lot to talk about!

When Nurse Maude had been a district nurse for almost 20 years, a pandemic arrived in New Zealand. The end of the First World War saw influenza, or the flu, make its way quickly around the world and millions of people died. Nurse Maude set up in Christchurch's Cathedral Square and helped hundreds of people every day. She was in charge of the city's relief centre and organised lists of patients for volunteers to visit.

Nurse Maude was recognised as one of the volunteers who had contributed the most to solving the crisis caused by the pandemic. Because of this, Christchurch City Council decided to give money every year to the Nurse Maude Association which meant they could afford to employ two more nurses.

Thanks to Sybilla's vision, New Zealand has a District Nursing Service, and the Nurse Maude Association continues to provide care to people in their homes in the Canterbury, Nelson-Marlborough and Wellington regions, as well as in the Nurse Maude Care Home and Nurse Maude Hospice in Merivale, Christchurch.

Honouring Nurse Maude

In 1934, Governor-General Lord Bledisloe honoured Nurse Maude with an Order of the British Empire (OBE) for her decades of district nursing and homecare. That same year, she also received the King George V Silver Jubilee Medal.

When Nurse Sibylla Maude died on 12 July 1935, thousands of people lined the streets between Christ Church Cathedral and St Peter's Anglican Church Cemetery. At her grave, the waiata Piko Nei te Matenga was sung, and she was farewelled with the words 'Mahi pai, pono hoki' ('Well done thou good and faithful servant.')

Welcome to the pick-a-path! You can read this book in order by turning the pages, or you can let the pick-a-path send you somewhere else in the book. Turn the page to the next story and keep an eye out for the pick-a-path. Happy reading!

Hope Soars

The story of Peter Button

A boy was born next to the runway in Wellington back in 1929. His name was Peter Button and he grew up watching planes. Peter had a passion for flying because of that runway and he also liked to help out at the local fire station.

From Plumber to Pilot

Peter worked as a plumber. He didn't know how to fly a helicopter, which he thought was the only thing stopping him from fulfilling his vision. But Peter didn't let it stop him for long. Within seven years, he had learned to fly. He bought his first helicopter thanks to Mark Dunajtschik, and together with neurosurgeon Dr Russell Worth, the Life Flight Trust was established. Peter's vision was now a reality.

When he was a young man, Peter witnessed a disaster — the terrible sinking of the *Wahine* ferry.

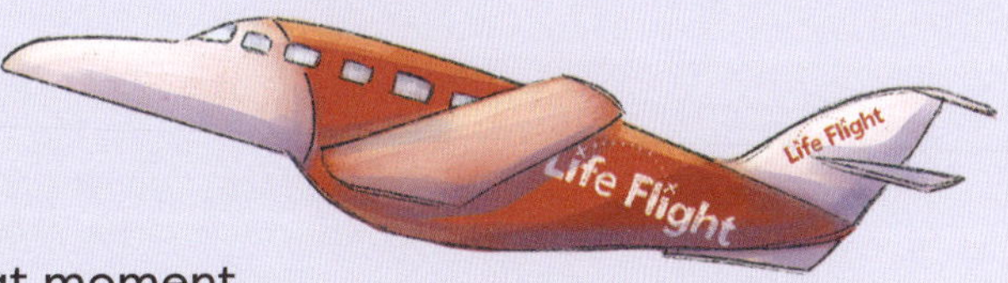

Everybody who was there tried to help. At that moment, Peter thought there had to be a better way. He had a vision — if he could have flown a helicopter to help with the rescue, he could have saved some of the lives that were lost that day. But, it was 1968 and rescue helicopters didn't exist in New Zealand yet.

Helicopter rescue missions are expensive, so in his free time, Peter would use the helicopter to raise money doing everything from scenic flights around Wellington to lifting pools into people's backyards!

In the early 1980s, he got a sponsorship deal with what is now Westpac bank. This meant he could dedicate one helicopter solely to rescue missions. It became the first Westpac Chopper.

In July 1986, the police boat *Lady Elizabeth II* capsized at the entrance to Wellington Harbour while on a training mission. Bravely, Peter decided to help. The wind was blowing very hard — over 100 kilometres per hour — and the waves were as tall as a three-storey building! Despite the conditions, Peter and his son, Clive, managed to save two of the four police officers from the monstrous waves.

Thanks to Peter's vision, Life Flight has helped rescue over 40,000 New Zealanders with their Westpac Choppers and fleet of Air Ambulance planes.

Peter and Clive Button were awarded a Queen's Gallantry Medal for bravery by Governor-General Sir Paul Reeves for their heroic actions after the capsize of the boat *Lady Elizabeth II*,

To read about someone getting a knighthood from Queen Elizabeth II, turn to Sir Ashley's story on page 41!

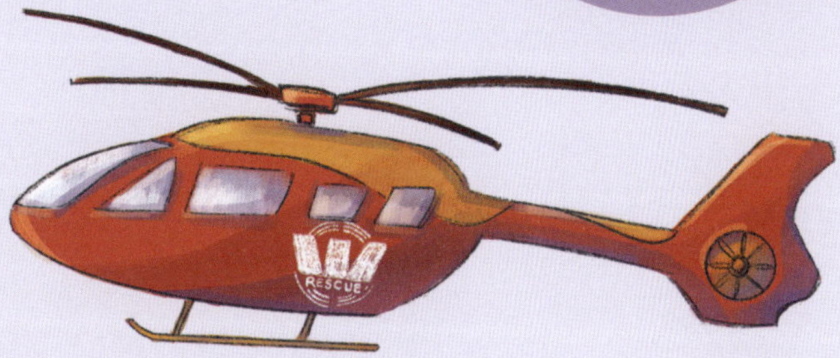

When Adults Think You're Sick Because You Saw a Cow

The story of Hannah Butler

Hannah Butler was two years old when her dad got a new job in a different country which meant her whole family had to move. The country they moved to was New Zealand — and they moved here over two hundred years ago!

When she was five, Hannah got sick. It was really scary for her and her family because no one knew what was wrong. There were no doctors or nurses, no hospitals or machines that could help figure out what was wrong. She couldn't speak. Her body kept moving in weird ways and she couldn't eat for days and days. No one had ever seen anything like it.

All the adults that Hannah's mum and dad knew kept trying to come up with ideas for what was wrong with Hannah. They tried giving her weird concoctions to make her better. One of the mixtures they gave her was rhubarb and water with burnt shells in it. It was an experiment.

It's been over 200 years, and still no one knows why Hannah got sick. Luckily, she got better but maybe no one will ever be able to figure out what was wrong with her.

What do you think New Zealand was like 200 years ago? Talk to your family about what it might have been like for Hannah. Do you think there were places Hannah could get medicine? Who do you think Hannah's parents could go to for help?

To learn about someone else with weird symptoms, turn to David's story on page 66!

Being Brave
The story of George Hamlin

When George Hamlin was born, his top lip had a big split in it up to his nose. Today we call this a cleft lip, and it can be seen on an ultrasound before a baby is born. But when George was born over 200 years ago, it would have been a big surprise to his mum and dad.

George lived with his parents in Waimate North, in a house that was quite far away from the nearest neighbours and there were no doctors around who could fix his lip. One day, his dad heard that a ship was visiting nearby with a surgeon on board. George and his dad travelled to Paihia to see if the surgeon could fix George's lip.

How do you think George and his dad travelled from Waimate North to Paihia? Maybe they had a horse, or maybe they walked all the way there! Have a look at a map and see if you can find Waimate North and Paihia (hint: they are in Northland).

The surgeon said he could do an operation and fix the split. It must have been scary for George, for someone to put pins in and sew up his face with no pain-killers. No one even knew about germs back then. They thought diseases and infections were caused by bad smells! They called this miasma. Imagine all the germs that must have got into George's face!

George was very brave. The operation was a success and after a few days one of the pins was removed from his face.

These days, when people need operations, they have them at the hospital. Sometimes if they are small procedures, they can be done by a local doctor.

Imagine if you needed an operation and you were taken to a ship instead!

To learn about an ambulance that flies patients through the sky to hospital, turn to the story about Starship Air Ambulance on page 50!

Being the First

The story of Jean Sandel

Jean Sandel moved around a bit when she was growing up. She was born in Gisborne, lived in Taumarunui when she was young, then went to high school in New Plymouth. When she was thinking about her future, she decided to become a doctor. That meant moving again – this time to Dunedin to go to the University of Otago.

Jean was born over 100 years ago when girls were just starting to get the same opportunities as boys. She was very clever. Growing up, she was sometimes the first girl EVER to win certain awards. When she was older, she was sometimes the first woman to do some things, too.

Jean was quite short but she didn't want the tall people she worked with to bend over and hurt their backs, so when she was doing surgery, she would stand on a box!

When Jean finished school and became a doctor, she won a prize. It was a scholarship for her to travel to a different country and work. But it wasn't safe to travel because the world was at war, so Jean had to stay in New Zealand. Instead she started working as a doctor in Wellington Hospital.

As soon as the war was over, Jean was off overseas to use her scholarship. She moved to the United Kingdom and achieved some firsts there, too. Jean was proving she wasn't just the best in New Zealand; she was the best everywhere she went.

When Jean came home to New Zealand, she moved back to New Plymouth and worked at the hospital there. She was known to be a good surgeon and boss, and she expected the best from everyone who worked there. She wanted all the hospital's patients to get the best care they could, so all the doctors and nurses knew they had to work their hardest.

Jean was proof that women could be anything they wanted to be. Even a century ago when not many women were doctors, she didn't let that stop her. She spent a lot of time encouraging young women to study hard, to do the best they could, and she inspired generations of women into working in medicine. If you also want to work in medicine, Jean would be behind you every step of the way.

What were some things Jean did?

- She was the first girl at New Plymouth Girls' High School to get a diploma from the Royal Life Saving Society.
- She won the Senior Scholarship in Medicine and the Scott Memorial Medal in 1936.
- She won the Fowler Scholarship in 1937.
- In 1938, She won three awards! The A F J Mickle Prize, the William Ledingham Christie Medal, and the New Zealand Graduates' Clinical Prize.
- She won the Travelling Scholarship in 1939, when she graduated as a doctor.
- She became the first female surgical registrar in London.
- She was the first New Zealand woman appointed as a Fellow of the Royal College of Surgeons.

To learn about someone else who was doing amazing things when they were young, turn to Eddie's story on page 64!

Travelling the World to Help at Home

The story of Elizabeth Gunn

Elizabeth 'Lizzie' Gunn was born about 150 years ago in Dunedin. As a child, she watched her dad studying to become a dentist and learnt that school and education were important no matter how old you are.

Lizzie attended school in Timaru and Dunedin, and she went to university to learn to become a doctor in three different cities around the world – Dunedin in Aotearoa, Edinburgh in Scotland, and Dublin in Ireland! When she was fully qualified, Lizzie came home and started working as a GP (general practitioner) in Wellington.

She had been a doctor for six years when the First World War began. Lizzie wanted to help the soldiers, but back in those days lots of people thought women couldn't do a job like that. She went and talked to the Prime Minister, William Massey. She told him she was just as qualified as any male doctor, and it wasn't fair to exclude her because she was a woman.

As a captain in the New Zealand Medical Corps (pronounced core), Lizzie worked at a measles hospital in Trentham. She did her job very well and was sent to Egypt on a ship with New Zealand soldiers.

Lizzie remembered her dad's interest in teeth. She had learnt a lot from him, which helped when she was working with children, their parents, and schools. She started something called a 'toothbrush drill' and got children to drink milk to help their teeth grow healthy and strong.

Lizzie decided that an easy way to teach kids how to be healthy was to bring them all together at a camp. Her first ever camp was at Turakina and there were 55 kids – they exercised, ate healthy foods and brushed their teeth. Her camp did so well that camps all around the country were started!

Lizzie was so good at her job that she got to be in charge of the Division of School Hygiene, as part of the government's Health Department! No one told her that a woman couldn't do that job – she had already proved she could.

Has anyone ever told you that boys and girls can't do the same things? That is not true! You can be interested in anything and have any job you want if you're curious and willing to work hard.

To learn about a doctor who looked after babies and their mums, turn to the story about Sir Graham on page 34!

Snow Bound for Tapanui

The story of Peter Snow

When Peter Snow was born, his sister, Betty, was already 10 years old. He was the baby of the family. Peter's mum died when he was young, and his sister helped raise him. Every day, they explored their neighbourhood in Auckland. When they moved to New Plymouth, they spent their days exploring there, too. Peter and Betty had a dog who sometimes joined them on their adventures.

Peter's favourite thing about school was playing rugby league. He did okay in class, but he wasn't the best student in maths, or English or science. He preferred being outside.

When he needed a job, Peter decided to be a lab technician even though he wasn't the best at science. He moved to the West Coast of the South Island and met his wife there – she was a physiotherapist.

Peter was good at his job and people noticed. Someone told Peter he should think about being a doctor, so at 30 years old, Peter went to medical school. He and his wife moved to Dunedin and for the five or six years he was in medical school, he was one of the oldest people in his classes. His wife kept working as a physiotherapist to make sure they could pay all their bills while Peter studied.

Peter worked all over the bottom of the South Island as a doctor – in Gore, the Catlins and Tapanui. He worked in Tapanui for ages – more than 30 years!

In 1984, a lot of people went to see Peter. They were tired, had headaches, couldn't sleep and their bodies hurt. It was almost like they all had the flu, but no one could figure out what was wrong! Peter brought some other doctors in to help him research. Their names were Dr Marion Poore and Dr Charlotte Paul.

They found out that all the people that went to see Peter had chronic fatigue syndrome – and Peter was the first doctor in New Zealand to diagnose it. People from around the world came to visit Peter because he was considered the expert in this new medical condition.

Even though Peter was now a world expert, he still worked every day as a doctor for the people of Tapanui. There were no rescue helicopters in those days, so if something went wrong, Peter was often the first person on the scene. He helped people who had accidents on the roads, in the forests and on farms. He saw a lot of accidents on farms and worked really hard to make farms safer places to work.

Peter loved being a doctor and helping people, but he also loved painting, and he loved thinking about space and meteorites. In the centre of Tapanui is a memorial to Peter — a moon rock.

Tapanui Flu

Another name for chronic fatigue syndrome is myalgic encephalomyelitis — a huge name! See if you can figure out how to pronounce it.

The newspapers called it 'Tapanui Flu' and a lot of people around New Zealand didn't believe it was real. Can you imagine being the first person to get sick with a new disease or condition, and no one believing it's real? How scary would that be!

To learn about someone else who played league, turn to Dave's story on page 56!

Health Innovation

Did you know the first-ever disposable syringe was invented right here in New Zealand? And today, Kiwi-led companies like MARS Bioimaging and Toku Eyes are making waves worldwide with their amazing innovations. I bet you can't wait to read more!

Forged by the Mountain

The story of William Pike

When William Pike was a boy, his grandad took him to Te-Hāwere-a-Maki | Goat Island Marine Reserve. He already loved nature and the outdoors, but the marine reserve showed him that there was a whole world underwater that was really cool.

William played a sport called water polo when he was at school. He wasn't the best person on the team but that's what a team is for – when everyone works together, they can do better than just one person working alone. William's team ended up being the best team in New Zealand three years in a row!

When William grew up, he got a job as a teacher. He had a friend called James who worked at the same school as him, and one school holiday they decided to climb a volcano: Mount Ruapehu.

Mount Ruapehu is a volcano

Did you know that Mount Ruapehu is the biggest active volcano in Aotearoa? It has three main peaks that are named Tahurangi, Te Heuheu and Paretetaitonga. In te reo Māori, Ruapehu means 'exploding pit' or 'pit of noise' — both excellent names for a volcano, don't you think?

William and James climbed all day, and by nighttime they made it to a hut that was only 600 metres away from Ruapehu's crater. That night, the volcano erupted. It roared like a plane and William got out of bed to see what was making all the noise. He opened the door just as mud, rocks and water were crashing down the mountain, and he got trapped.

It was very scary for William — he was stuck, his leg hurt, and he was on an erupting volcano. James helped William get as comfortable as he could before running down the mountain for help. He found a worker and told them that his friend was trapped and hurt.

Rescuers came to the hut and dug William out. He was freezing and injured, so they needed to work as fast as they could. They got him down the mountain, into a rescue helicopter and to Taumarunui Hospital. When he got there he smelled like sulphur and was covered head to toe in duck feathers which had come out of his jacket.

After he had been stabilised, they transferred him into another helicopter and he was taken to Waikato Hospital for surgery.

When William woke up, he was shocked to see that one of his legs was missing. But after a few moments, he thought about how lucky he was to be alive, and that was more important than having two legs.

William thought about his future as an amputee, and what he wanted to achieve. He wanted to walk again, be a teacher again and to be able to climb mountains again.

But first, he needed to heal and learn how to live with one leg instead of two. He had friends and family who helped him, and who listened when he needed someone to talk to. They inspired him to keep going when he was having a hard time.

William wanted to keep living his life; to mow his lawns, go to the beach, go on bushwalks. He had a prosthetic foot, but he kept getting sand, dust and dirt in it. He had to get it cleaned out all the time and have repairs done to keep the foot working.

One day William had an idea — if he could cover his foot with something, this would keep it from getting filled with stuff that was damaging it. William invented a cover for prosthetic feet called PRO ARMOUR® and he now sells them all over the world. The cover gives amputees the confidence to live their lives and keep doing the activities they enjoy.

William's life was changed the day he climbed Mount Ruapehu. But thanks to his inner strength and the support of those around him, he didn't let anything stand in the way of achieving his goals.

Preparing young people for the world

The William Pike Challenge is all about inspiring people to unlock their confidence and step outside their comfort zones. The challenge has five outdoor activities, 20 hours of community service and 20 hours of passion projects. It aims to build resilience, teamwork, relationships, connections and key life skills. The Challenge has transformed over 30,000 lives with hundreds of schools around Aotearoa having participated.

To learn about someone else whose life was changed by a mountain, turn to Corey's story on page 60!

The World's First Disposable Syringe

The story of Colin Murdoch

Colin Murdoch grew up in Christchurch. His dad was a pharmacist, and his mum was a homemaker. Colin liked to experiment with things, and by the time he was a teenager he had started inventing. Although he enjoyed it, he never thought of doing it for a job. He wanted to be a doctor but like his dad and both his brothers, he trained to become a pharmacist.

Colin moved from Christchurch to Timaru to start his own pharmacy. After work and on the weekends, he did things he loved, like hunting and going to the movies. He was even friends with the owner of a movie theatre! Colin never stopped creating and inventing new things.

Did you know that New Zealanders used to be considered British back in the day? Even though he was born in Christchurch, Colin had a British passport. Once he was even featured on a list of British inventors!

Have you ever had an injection? Before Colin's invention, doctors and nurses would use metal syringes that needed to be cleaned before the next injection. The stuff in the injection was stored in glass and sometimes it would break and the liquid would go everywhere! If you have ever had an injection, Colin's plastic syringe is the reason it is so fast and safe.

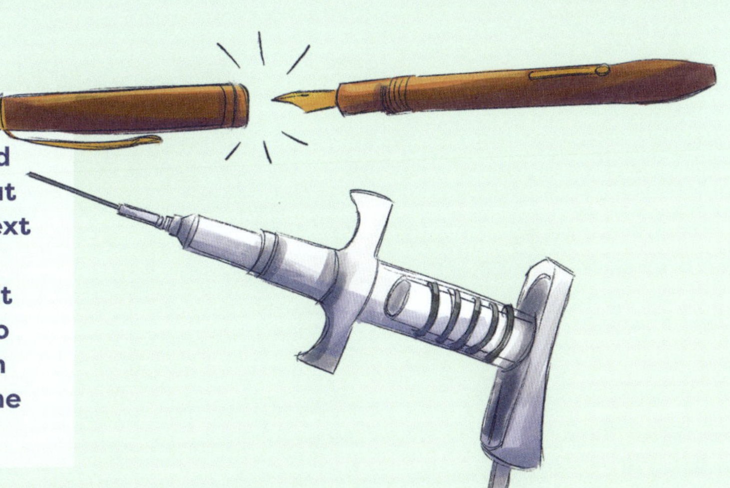

One day, he was on a plane from Auckland to Christchurch when he pulled the cap off his pen and had a brainwave — 'Eureka!' — Colin had just thought of something that would change the world — the disposable plastic syringe.

Colin invented so many things. He invented things for hunting, farming and medicine. He would wake up in the night and scribble his ideas onto some paper next to his bed so he didn't forget them in the morning. Colin started travelling the world, testing and improving his inventions. Over the years, Colin worked for a number of different companies, designing products and solving problems. The companies he worked for made lots of the money from his inventions. Others even stole his design for the plastic syringe and started making and selling them!

No one at home in New Zealand really knew what Colin was doing. They didn't know he was changing the world with his inventions but a lot of people realise it now. One of Colin's inventions was put on a stamp, and now kids at school do projects about him.

Colin's wife, Marilyn, was one of the main reasons he could travel the world and invent. They met at the movies one day. She was checking people's tickets, and his friend had asked him if he could check tickets, too. They got married not long afterwards, and started their family. While Colin was travelling Marilyn looked after their four children at home which was a lot of work!

What is a pharmacist? Turn to Leanne's story on page 46 to learn about what a pharmacist does.

The Parthemore Pulley

The story of Lorraine Parthemore

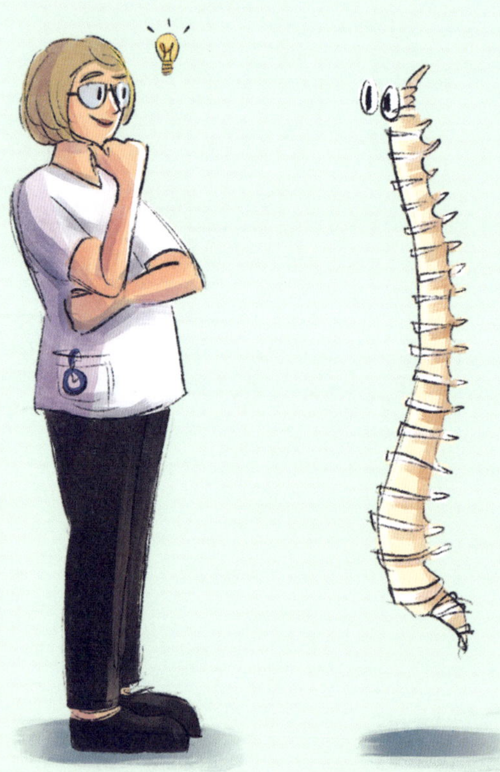

Lorraine Parthemore grew up in south Taranaki on a large farm. She had four brothers and sisters. The farm was their playground, and the lambs and calves were their pets. Not many people lived nearby, so there were only 18 other kids at Lorraine's school!

She spent her days making kites and flying them on the farm, building treehouses and making go-karts. There was always something to be built out of stuff lying around.

When she was five years old, Lorraine decided she wanted to be a nurse. She finished primary school and high school, then went to nursing school. When she finished her training she moved to Texas in America. Lorraine thought she would only be away from New Zealand for a year, but she stayed there for 14 years!

When Lorraine came home, she got a job working with an orthopaedic surgeon (someone who looks after muscles and bones). She helped the surgeon with operations and one day, she noticed a problem with how the operating theatre was set up. She then had a brainwave that led to an invention.

She thought that surely someone else had already invented something that could help but after looking all over the internet and talking to hospitals all over the North Island she realised there was nothing! So, Lorraine started sketching her invention.
She talked to a company in Auckland about

Living in a different country

Do you think you could live in a different country for as long as Lorraine? What do you think would be different? Do you think they might speak a different language than you? Or eat different foods?

making her invention come to life. She sent them her sketches and worked with them to tweak the design, then one day a courier arrived with a parcel — her invention! She took it into work with her, attached it to the bed for surgery, and it worked amazingly well. The surgeon said they should name it the Parthemore Pulley.

Being an inventor

Lorraine says that if you have an idea, go with it! Draw it, write it down and keep working on it. Anyone can be an inventor if they see something in the world they could improve. If you don't try, you will never know if you could invent something that could change the world.

It was really hard for Lorraine to get her invention into hospitals all by herself. She knew teamwork would make it easier, so she started working with a company in Nelson. Lorraine didn't care about being recognised for her invention around the world — she just wanted to help people.

Lorraine has been a nurse for over 50 years. Her sketch and the prototype (first version) of her invention are so important they're in a museum. How cool is that?

To learn about another nurse making a big difference, turn to Tania's story on page 48!

MARS Calling

The story of Anthony Butler

Anthony Butler was curious. He had always been curious, even when he was young, but didn't know what to do with all his curiosity. One of his teachers told him he should be a doctor. Anthony thought that could be interesting, so he shrugged and went to medical school to become one. His sister was there, too.

While learning to be a doctor, Anthony still wasn't sure if it was what he wanted to do with his life. He was still really curious about how the world worked, and liked maths and physics, so he started to study those subjects as well. When he finished with school, he was a doctor who was able to do maths and physics, too. He had been very busy!

Anthony worked at a hospital and learnt how to take pictures of the inside of people — this is called radiology. He really liked how medicine and technology worked together to make these images. Anthony thought if only he knew a bit more, he could improve the machines. He was also curious about how computers can understand pictures of the human body so he went back to university to become a Doctor of Computer Engineering, too.

Anthony's curiosity led him to study so many subjects. He could be a doctor, a computer engineer, a radiologist and a physicist — like his dad.

On holiday in Switzerland, Anthony went to look at a huge physics machine that was trying to find a particle called the Higgs Boson. He wondered whether parts of this machine could be useful in hospitals. He found that if you measure each particle, called photons, that make up an X-ray beam, you can turn the image from black and white into colour. He finally knew what he wanted to do!

Measuring photons is really hard work because they are so small and move fast, and there are so many of them in an X-ray. Anthony and his

What is radiology?

Radiology uses machines to take images of the inside of your body. You can see bones, muscles, organs, veins and arteries. You can even see babies before they're born! One of the ways to make these images is called x-ray. An x-ray shoots beams of light called photons into your body and makes an image in black and white.

dad had to figure out how to measure them in a way that would work for doctors. Luckily, Anthony had lots of ideas because he had learnt so much. They started a company called MARS Bioimaging and adapted all sorts of new technology — like robotics and microchips — to help measure photons one at a time.

Anthony and a group of experts have now invented machines that can be used in hospitals to make these coloured images. He thinks it would be really cool to make these machines for ambulances, too, so that in an emergency, an ambulance team can find what's wrong as fast as possible.

This technology is still pretty new. If you need a scan in a hospital, chances are it will still be in black and white. But one day, coloured images will be in hospitals everywhere, and Anthony will have helped doctors diagnose patients all around the world.

Coloured images can help doctors so much with figuring out what's wrong in someone's body. The bones, muscles and organs come out different colours because the photons in the beam of light hit them differently. If there is a problem in a bone, that part of the bone also changes colour — same with muscles and organs.

To learn about another health hero who was told he should be a doctor, turn to Peter Snow's story on page 18!

Inventing Cool Products to Improve Care for Patients

The story of Fisher & Paykel Healthcare

Fisher & Paykel Healthcare has been around for a really long time. They make products to help people feel better, and during the COVID-19 pandemic, these products were used to help millions of people all around the world. It all started in Auckland.

Over 50 years ago, way back in 1969, a doctor and two engineers were trying to find a way to help sick people at Auckland City Hospital. They ended up inventing a machine that helped people breathe better. It was called a humidifier. Their prototype was made using just a jar from the kitchen!

Fisher & Paykel Healthcare help people all around the world. Their products can be used on everyone from tiny newborn babies to your mum, dad, nana, koro, or even their mums, dads, nanas and koro.

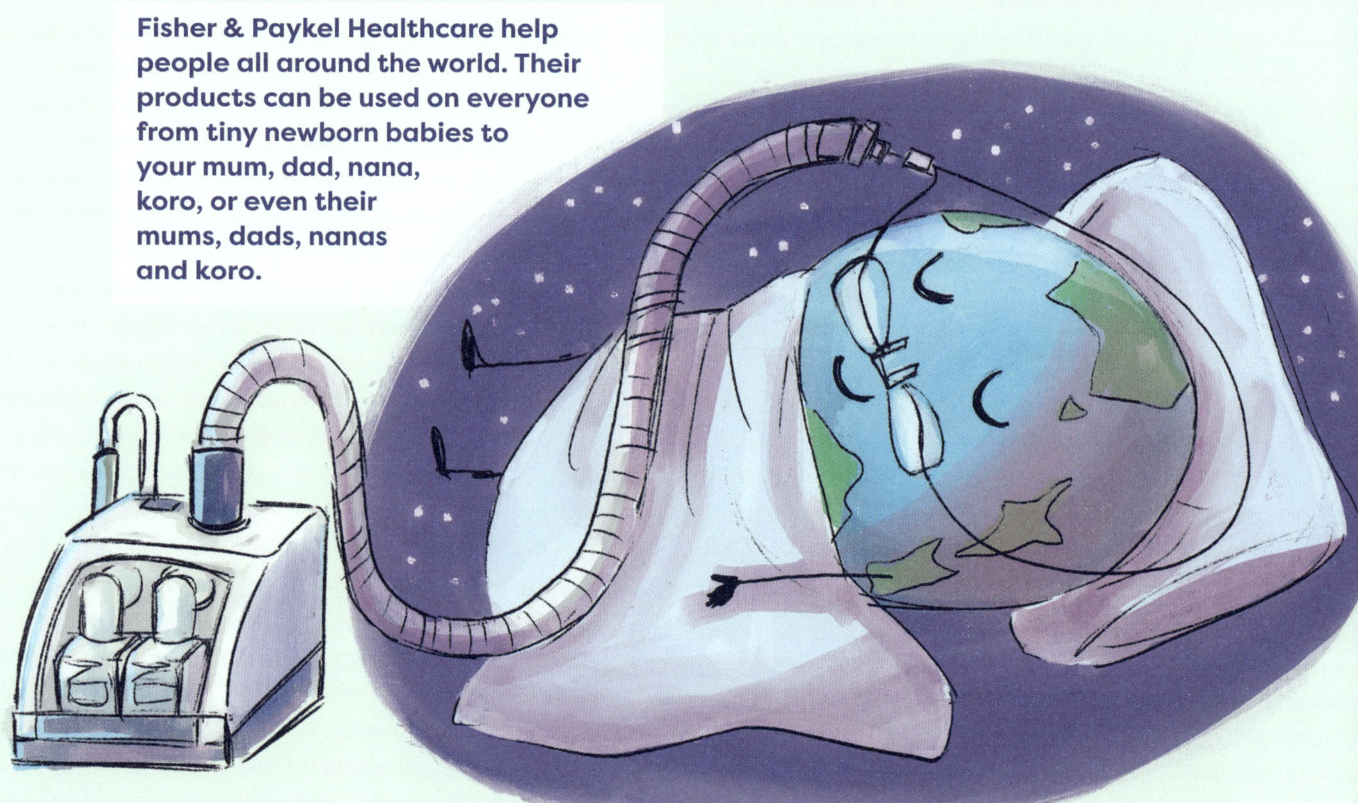

Fisher & Paykel Healthcare still makes lots of different machines that help people breathe. Some people use them in hospital, while others use their products at home, to help them sleep.

These days, there are lots of people working for Fisher & Paykel Healthcare. Some are doctors, engineers or office workers. Some are people who load boxes into trucks to be shipped all around the world. They are one of the biggest companies in Aotearoa!

Being a health hero doesn't just mean being a doctor. Everyone, no matter their job, can help improve people's quality of life.

How does Fisher & Paykel Healthcare know what to make?

1. **Engineers talk to doctors and nurses to find out what problems their patients have that need solving.**
2. **The engineers design a new product and create a prototype in the lab.**
3. **The new product gets tested by doctors and nurses and the engineers watch people use the product to see if it needs any improvements.**
4. **When the design is perfect and people are ready to buy the product, Fisher & Paykel Healthcare create a factory line.**
5. **The factory workers assemble all the products and ship them around the world.**

To learn about another cool inventor, turn to the story about Sid Yarrow on page 38!

I Care

The story of Ehsan Vaghefi

Normally, people are born with two eyes but sometimes those eyes don't work as they are meant to. This can happen from birth, or they can work for a while and then stop.

Ehsan was born in Iran. When he was born, his dad's eyes hadn't worked in a long time. He was blind and had been since he was young. Eshan's grandfather couldn't afford to get a doctor to look at his dad's eyes so he lost his sight because of a medical condition. Growing up, Ehsan spent a lot of time with people who were blind or had a blind parent. He always knew that when he grew up he wanted to work with eyes.

Moving to different countries to reach your dream

Eshan heard about someone in Australia who was trying to create an artificial (fake) eye that could use a camera to talk to the brain also known as a bionic eye. He moved to Australia to help and learn as much as he could. Then Ehsan saw a project that looked pretty cool in Aotearoa which was about trying to find eye disease as fast as possible. What's better than helping someone whose eyes have stopped working? Figuring out the problem and fixing it before their eyes stop working in the first place.

Ehsan moved to New Zealand and worked at the University of Auckland for a long time. He got really good at his job and taught lots of other people about eyes, too.

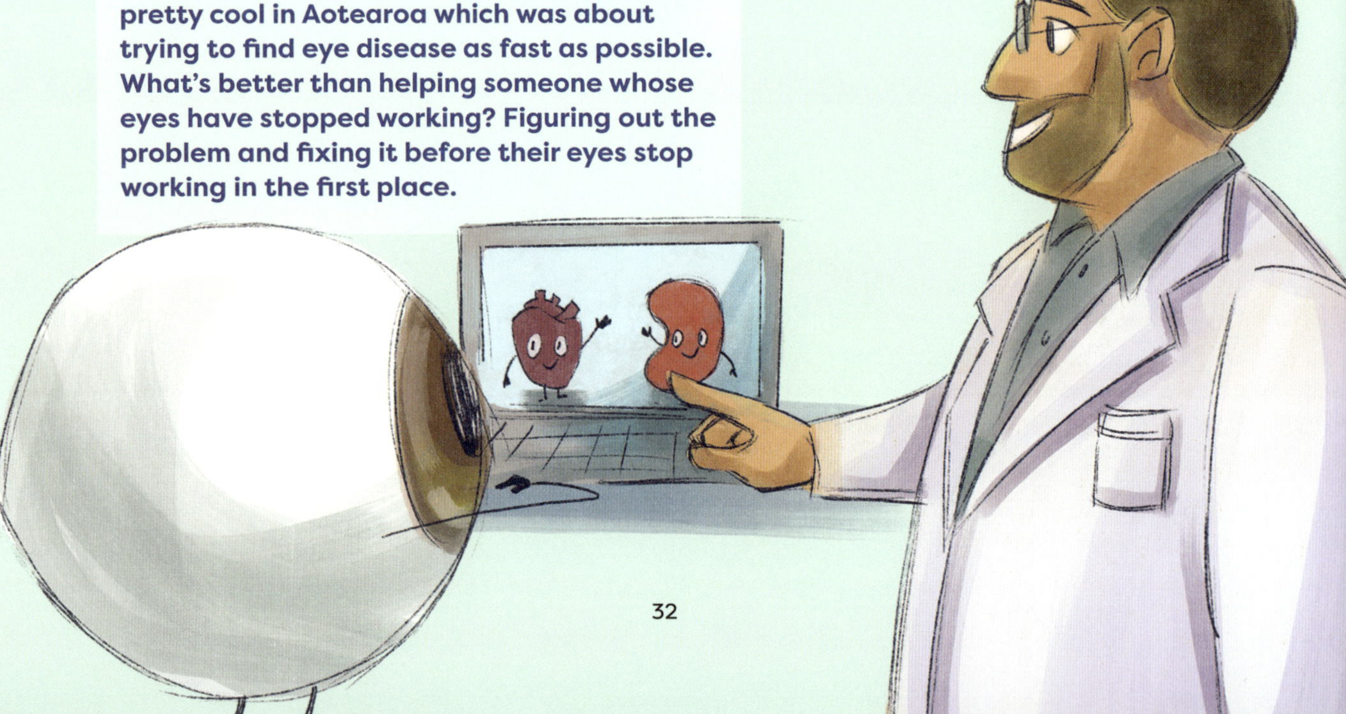

Did you know a doctor can find problems with your heart through your eyes? And problems with your kidneys, too? Eshan worked with an ophthalmologist (an eye doctor) named David Squirrell and they started Toku Eyes, to create machines that scan your eyes and find problems in your body.

Someone believed in Toku Eyes so much they gave Ehsan and David money to make their eye-scanning machines. They called one CLAiR. CLAiR can find all sorts of health problems and has scanned over a million eyes!

To fulfil his childhood goal, Ehsan had to leave New Zealand and move to America. This is the fifth country he has lived in while working to achieve his goal. He still works for the University of Auckland, though, and we think of him as a great Kiwi.

Ehsan has spent his life trying to make sure eye health checks are affordable and available to everyone.

Travelling around different countries to reach your dream

Ehsan travelled to other countries for weeks at a time, having meetings with people and trying to inspire them with what Toku Eyes could do. He tried to get them interested in giving money to help build the eye-scanning machines. Sometimes he had to sleep in airports because he didn't have enough time to go to hotels and sleep in a bed.

To learn about someone else who worked really hard to achieve his dream, turn to the story about Rob's Heart-Stopping Moments on page 54!

Monty the Mouse
The story of Sir Graham Liggins

Just over 100 years ago, a curious and smart boy was born in Thames. His parents named him Graham, but he loved a cartoon called Monty the Mouse so much that everyone called him Mont.

Mont was interested in the world around him and loved exploring and figuring out how things worked. He decided to become a doctor because that was a job where he could spend his whole life learning.

Mont started working as a GP, then went overseas to learn more about being a doctor. When he came home to Aotearoa, he was qualified as a doctor for mums and babies and was really interested in doing more research to help them. Mont looked at mums and babies to find something he could help them with. He decided to research premature labour.

Mont discovered what caused premature labour in sheep, which is pretty cool, but humans don't go into labour in the same way. Still to this day, no one has figured out why some babies are born early.

While he was working with sheep, he found out how to make babies' lungs grow faster. This discovery changed the world and saved the lives of so many premature babies.

What is premature labour?

Labour is what we call it when a mum's body is ready and starts to deliver their baby. The baby has grown as much as they can inside their mum, and they are ready to come out into the world. Sometimes, a mum's body gets ready too early, which is called premature labour. Sometimes babies are born too early, when their bodies haven't finished growing. They might need help at the hospital, and they can stay in hospital for weeks or even months until their bodies have grown enough to work properly at home.

Mont spent his life being curious, exploring all the ways problems might be solved. Sometimes, like Mont, you might not get the answers you're looking for, but you could discover something that changes the world along the way.

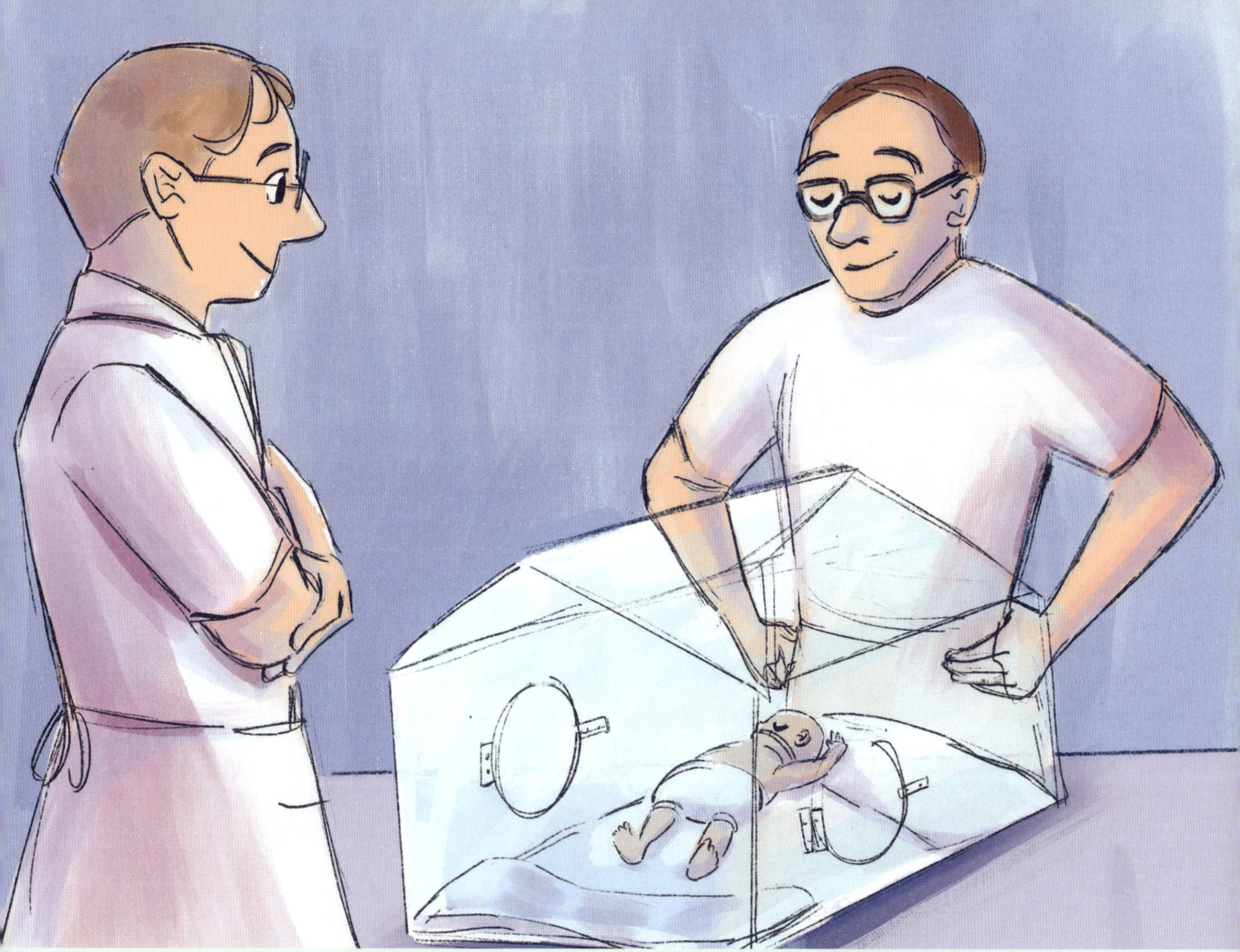

Corticosteroids

Mont discovered that baby lambs' lungs were more developed than baby humans. He did an experiment on a mother sheep by giving her an injection before she gave birth to her lamb. The injection was a corticosteroid (cor-ti-co-STEER-oid) and it helped the lamb's lungs develop faster. This meant even if a lamb was born early, its lungs were better at breathing.

To learn about someone whose parents were worried about him when he was born, turn to George's story on page 13!

Gene Detective

The story of Parry Guilford

When Parry Guilford was young, he wanted to be a chemist. Not because he knew what they did, but because he thought the word was cool. Then he saw a picture of a virus stuck on the side of bacteria in a book and thought that was even cooler. This tiny, weirdly-shaped thing that causes lots of diseases was stuck to this other tiny, weirdly-shaped thing that causes lots of other diseases! And the virus was putting its DNA into the bacteria to multiply itself.

Parry thought this was so fascinating that he wanted to do it as a job when he grew up. He became a medical researcher, which is kind of like being a detective.

He spends his days looking for clues, just like a detective. He's spent years looking for clues about a really bad disease in people's stomachs called cancer. Sometimes, our DNA tells our bodies that because people in our families have been sick, our bodies should get sick, too. Parry wanted to find out how to stop our bodies from doing that.

Parry searched and searched, and he and his team managed to find the gene that was being passed from parents to their children and making their stomachs sick. He's helped make so many people better – grandparents, mums, dads, and children.

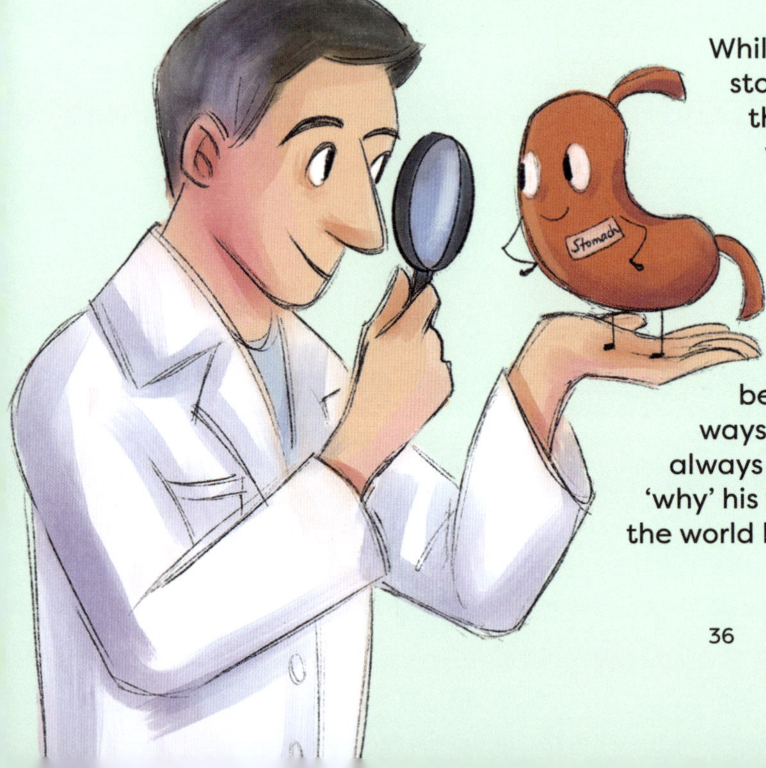

While he was researching, he grew little stomachs in the lab so they could test the medicines and see if they were working. Some were as small as a pea!

Now that he's done his job for a while, he still thinks it's cool. But he thinks helping people who are sick is an even better reason to do his job. He doesn't think you should ever stop being a detective and looking for new ways to help people. He thinks you should always keep asking 'why'. He's been asking 'why' his whole life, and has travelled around the world helping people.

What is a virus?

A virus is very small, made of organic material, and causes diseases in animals and plants as well as humans. It is made up of protein and genetic material. Viruses include things like COVID-19, chicken pox and the flu, which can't be treated with antibiotics.

What are bacteria?

Bacteria (or bacterium if there is only one) are bigger than viruses, but still very small. You can only see them under a microscope. They are all through your body and are found in plants and animals, too. Some bacteria are good, but some can make you sick. They are made up of only one cell. Sometimes they join together and make different shapes like spirals, rods and circles. Bacteria can cause illness such as salmonella, tetanus and strep throat. You can treat bacterial infections with antibiotics.

What is DNA?

Deoxyribonucleic acid (DNA) makes up all living things. Everyone has their own DNA – it is what makes you unique. It's like the instructions that tell your body how to make you, you. Every living thing has DNA, including plants and animals, and even viruses and bacteria. Genes, which you get from your parents, are made up of DNA.

To learn about someone with a disease that people have been researching for ages, turn to Anna's story on page 62!

The Machine with NO Instructions

The story of Sid Yarrow

Sid Yarrow worked as a lab technician at Green Lane Hospital in Auckland during one of the most important and exciting moments in New Zealand medical history – when the first EVER open-heart surgery on a human took place. These days this operation happens every day in hospitals all around the world, but Sid helped make sure the first one in New Zealand was a success – and he had only lived here for four years when he did it.

What's a lab technician?

A lab technician, or lab tech, is someone whose job is to set up and test equipment, tools and machines. In a hospital, they set things up for doctors and nurses. If something isn't working, the lab tech is the person that can fix it. Lab techs do a lot of other jobs as well and can also work in science labs!

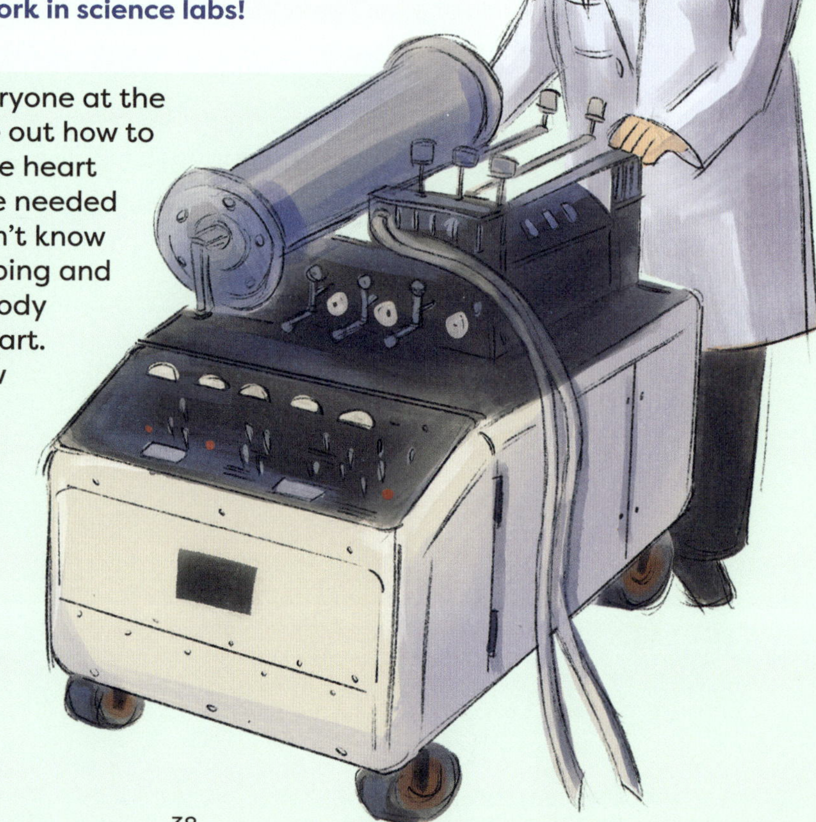

All the way back in 1957 everyone at the hospital was trying to figure out how to help a 10-year-old girl whose heart wasn't working properly. She needed a long surgery, but they didn't know how to keep her blood pumping and taking oxygen around her body while they worked on her heart. They decided to order a new machine all the way from the United Kingdom. It was called the Melrose Heart-Lung Machine.

When it arrived, it came in a big wooden box with no instructions! How was Sid meant to put it together?

He wrote a letter to Melrose and asked for the instructions. They sent him a diagram, but it wasn't very helpful, and Sid was still confused about what all the different parts did and where they went. He threw the parts away when he couldn't figure out what they did.

Sid, along with Brian Barratt-Boyes and Alfred Melville, worked hard to make the machine even better than Melrose, and they designed a new feature! They added a part that meant they could control how much oxygen the young girl would get from the machine. This meant they could give her the right amount of oxygen.

Once they had put the machine together with all its new and improved parts, they had to figure out how to kill all the germs on it so that it was safe to use in surgery. They couldn't heat it to kill the germs because some of the parts would melt!

Sid knew that there was a new way to kill the germs being used in Australia. Instead of heat, it used a gas called ethylene oxide. But where was he meant to find that? There was none in New Zealand, so Sid asked a hospital in Sydney if he could use some of their gas.

Who were Brian and Alfred?

Sir Brian Barratt-Boyes was a pioneering New Zealand cardiothoracic (heart and lungs) surgeon. He performed the first open-heart surgery in New Zealand and was one of the first surgeons in the world to put pacemakers in to help people's hearts.

Alfred Melville was an engineer and inventor. He thought that making New Zealand's medical tools better was happening too slowly, so he started inventing. He created the first dehumidifier prototype and was the person to make the parts needed to improve the Melrose Heart-Lung Machine.

After a lot of trial and error, Sid and the rest of the team got it all sorted. Brian did the surgery with help from his team, and the young girl's heart was made better. She was very brave for having the surgery since it had never been done before.

The Melrose Heart-Lung Machine is now part of the museum collection at MOTAT in Auckland. Sometimes it is on display in the museum and sometimes it is in storage to make sure that it is looked after properly. If you visit MOTAT you might get to see it!

To learn about something else that has saved a lot of lives, turn to the story about Peter Button on page 10!

Health Care

Every day, people across Aotearoa put their heart and soul into caring for our health and we have so much to thank them for. From nursing to research to growing healthy food, we have some incredible stories to share!

1. **Blooming Marvellous:** The story of Sir Ashley Bloomfield
2. **The World is Your Oyster:** The story of Catherine Bell
3. **A Helping Hand for Health:** The story of Leanne Te Karu
4. **Finding Tania:** The story of Tania Mullane
5. **Starship to the Rescue:** The story of Starship National Air Ambulance
6. **A Breath of Fresh Air:** The story of Jim Bartley

Blooming Marvellous

The story of Sir Ashley Bloomfield

Ashley Bloomfield comes from Maraenui in Napier. When he was young, he thought he might become a pilot. After a visit to Wellington Hospital when he was 14, he thought he would become a doctor instead. But what he became, when Aotearoa needed him most, was the Director-General of Health.

Although Ashley liked science when he was at school and was good at it, there were definitely others who were better than him. When he talked to someone about going to medical school, they didn't know if they were going to let him in. Luckily, Ashley got into the University of Auckland where he started learning how to be a doctor.

After three years at medical school, Ashley took a year off to travel the world. He hitchhiked around Europe and did all sorts of jobs. He worked as a labourer, a waiter and a farmer. He had a great time that year and came home with a lot of new skills.

While he was studying, Ashley also joined the New Zealand Defence Force's (NZDF) territorial force and trained as an officer. Ashley says that his time there helped him learn how to be a better leader and keep calm under pressure.

There are a lot of different jobs you can do as a doctor. Ashley decided he'd try clinical medicine and worked in hospitals. He liked it but realised it might not be the right job for him, so, he gave public health medicine a go. His parents were pretty worried he wouldn't find the right job. When he finished learning how to work in public health, Ashley decided to spend half a year working at the Ministry of Health | Manatū Hauora. He enjoyed this job and ended up working there for over 20 years.

After he finished medical school and became a doctor, Ashley realised that during his year travelling, he had learnt how to work with and understand lots of different people – a very important skill to have when you're a doctor.

Ashley worked as a manager and advisor, and he moved to France with his family for a year to work for the World Health Organisation (WHO). To get to work, Ashley would have to cross the border of France into Switzerland!

A little while after missing out on a job he applied for, Ashley got a call about a new job at Capital & Coast District Health Board (CCDHB). This was a good job and after a few years Ashley's dad rang him and told him he should apply for a job at the Hutt Valley DHB. His dad went with him to his pōwhiri when he started there.

It was the job he didn't get that set him on the path to becoming the Director-General of Health. New Zealand was so lucky he didn't get that job!

Every day, Ashley got to talk to people in the community: doctors, whānau and patients. He would cycle along the river to and from work. He had ridden his bike a lot in Europe and liked that he could cycle to work in New Zealand, too.

Working with the DHB made Ashley confident enough to apply for the job of Director-General of Health. He got the job just in time to help guide Aotearoa through the COVID-19 pandemic. During the first six weeks of the pandemic, Ashley would wake up in a cold sweat at 3am wondering why COVID-19 had happened while he was in charge.

'When COVID-19 came along and pushed me probably beyond what I thought I could do . . . when physically and mentally and emotionally . . . you're on the edge and you're tired and you've worked all night . . . you still have to remain leaderful and calm, thinking not just about yourself but about the people you're responsible for.'

Public health is all about working together

Public health is about building trust. If the public is being asked to do something different to what they are used to, they need to trust whoever is asking or telling them to do it. If your mum or dad, sister, brother, teacher, or another member of your whānau asked you to do something, would you do it? Why?

In exchange, the health system needs to understand people and how they live. Instructions need to be accessible, explained well and necessary. If both sides are doing their jobs well, it builds trust and gives people the power to take ownership of their health and the health of their whānau. If you tell someone you need a drink of water, do they listen and get you one? Why? Because they know what you need and want to help.

Every day for months, Ashley was on TV at 1pm alongside the Prime Minister. His calm and careful manner helped to guide and reassure people through the pandemic. He was bombarded with questions every day by journalists at the briefing, and every day he had the answers – or if he didn't, he would say he didn't know and promise to get the information.

Ashley knew it was important that we could see him on TV each day to show the country he was a trustworthy public figure. By being good at his job, by being honest and reliable, Ashley showed that he could be trusted.

Ashley became a doctor. He didn't become a pilot. He spends a lot of time on planes for work, but he would still like to learn how to fly a plane himself one day.

'I'm so convinced that we had the most amazing people, and New Zealand responded so fantastically . . . You can't police a lockdown. It relies on everybody understanding and accepting the rationale, and having a collective sense of purpose, and that's why I think we were successful . . . We prevented literally 15–20,000 deaths and the impact that would have had on whānau and communities.'

To find a story about another doctor who served in the New Zealand Defence Force, turn to the story about Elizabeth 'Lizzie' on page 16!

The World is Your Oyster

The story of Catherine Bell

When Catherine Bell was growing up, her dad grew food in their garden. Some of the plants grew so tall! She could see the stalks of corn growing out her window! Her mum was a really good cook and liked to read cookbooks to learn all sorts of new ways to make food, so Catherine always had something interesting to eat.

When she was about to finish school, Catherine was looking for a job. She thought about becoming a kindergarten teacher, a nurse or working in an office. She decided to become a nurse. There were 50 people in her class, and a lot of other people wanted to be nurses, too!

Catherine learnt many important skills in her new job. She learnt how to care for people, how to be organised, how to work in a team. But she also learnt that she didn't want to be a nurse her whole life. She remembered her dad's garden and her mum's love of cooking and decided to go to cooking school in England.

When she came home to Aotearoa, Catherine and a friend bought a delicatessen in Auckland where they sold all sorts of different foods. After a few years, Catherine set up a cookware store and cooking school. She sold lots of different kitchen gadgets, and taught classes on how to use them, that would make cooking easier and more fun. She travelled the world finding brand new inventions for the kitchen, bringing them home and teaching people how to use them.

What you think you want to be when you grow up isn't what you have to be forever. You can grow and change, learn new things and try different jobs.

Then Catherine started writing. She wrote articles for magazines, and two of her own cookbooks. Then she decided to start her own magazine, all about food. She had so many jobs and was very busy!

Catherine started Garden to Table which teaches young people about gardening and cooking. She teaches kids where food comes from — whether it's grown in people's gardens, in Aotearoa or if it's grown somewhere else in the world and brought here. She teaches kids that growing and cooking fresh food is important, and good for your body. Packaged food can be okay, but the best food is made with love and shared with others.

What's your favourite food?

Is your favourite thing to eat a mix of different ingredients? How do you think it gets made? Do you think you could write the recipe down so that other people could learn to make it? Do the people in your family like the same foods as you?

To learn about a health hero who lived in another country before returning to Aotearoa, turn to Lorraine's story on page 26!

A Helping Hand for Health

The story of Leanne Te Karu

'What happens when you swallow a medicine?' Leanne Te Karu asked herself when she was young. 'How does it know where to go in your body to work?'

As a child, Leanne was familiar with doctors, pharmacists and medicine because her lungs didn't do their job properly and she got sick a lot. She didn't let that stop her from playing sports, though. Her passion took her all the way to America to play basketball! It was scary going from Tūrangi to a new country with a different culture, but Leanne was brave. She shared her Māori culture with others and learnt about their culture, too.

Leanne's dad asked her what she wanted to do when she finished playing basketball. She wanted to learn about medicines and how they work in the human body. Once Leanne knew what they did, she thought back to when she was a child wondering about such things, and decided to become a pharmacist.

What does a pharmacist do?

Pharmacists can be found working in many different places. Some work in community pharmacies, while others work in hospital pharmacies. Some do research, and others are teachers. Pharmacists can work for companies to make medicine, and in Aotearoa they can work with Māori or Pasifika health providers. They can give advice, and if they become prescribing pharmacists, they can write prescriptions, too. Pharmacists can also give immunisations. To learn all about the Kiwi who invented the plastic syringe, find Colin's story on page 24!

Leanne's first job was working at Waikato Hospital in the kidney ward. She saw a lot of people there whose health could have been better and sometimes, it was because they couldn't get the care they needed. They had so much to offer their whānau and communities, but their health was often in the way.

The more Leanne helped people, the more she noticed that her Māori patients would want to understand more about the medicine she was giving them and how it worked. Someone even travelled all the way to her house on horseback to ask her to explain the medical words on a letter they got from the hospital.

Medicines come from a lot of different sources. A lot were found in the nature around us. In Aotearoa, our native plants are really good for lots of things. Sometimes they can heal even better than chemicals made in a lab. Using native plants and mātauranga (knowledge, wisdom and skills) to heal is called Rongoā Māori.

She thought there must be more Māori pharmacists out there, but she didn't know them. She thought she'd start a group they could join. Lots of people didn't like that she had formed this group, and she got lots of letters that were really mean. But Leanne was brave. She kept going and eventually the letters started coming from people who wanted to join.

Leanne works on marae and in small towns around the country. She learns about people and their health and works to get them the best medicines she can. She knows that medicines can help when you are sick or stop you from getting sick in the first place. She also knows that they can cause problems if they are not the right ones or given in the right dosage.

Now she asks questions like: Have we got the right medicines in Aotearoa? Who is choosing them for the country? Can everyone in the country access them equally? And you know what? She's so good at her job that a few years ago, the government asked Leanne those questions, too.

Sometimes people are mean to others. Would you ever write someone a mean letter, email or text? How do you think they would feel if you were mean to them? How do you feel if someone is mean to you? Being mean isn't cool — you should be kind instead.

To learn about another amazing trailblazer, turn to Jean's story on page 14!

Finding Tania

The story of Tania Mullane

Tania Mullane is from Te Puke. When she was young, Tania had trouble with school – she didn't get the best marks, she wasn't very confident and she didn't know what she wanted to be when she grew up. She was adopted by her parents, and as the only Pasifika member of her family, Tania wasn't really sure where she fit in the world. When Tania was 16, her older sister worked as a nurse. Tania wasn't sure what she wanted to do, so she followed in her footsteps and became a nurse too.

When Tania finished nursing school, there weren't many jobs. Only three or four nurses from each class got jobs because there were just so many nurses. So Tania returned to Te Puke, unsure of what she was going to do next.

Tania's first job was on a marae. She took her baby to work with her each day and helped people learn new things.

Her next job was as a nurse for Whānau Āwhina Plunket where she worked for seven years.

Tania saw a cool job at a polytech – a school for adults. She applied for it but didn't get it.

Tania was disappointed, but she worked hard, and the next time she applied, she got the job.

At the polytech, Tania worked with some great leaders. She decided she wanted to be a leader, too. They told her she had to go back to school and continue her studies. It had been a very long time since she had been at school, and she didn't know if she would be any good. But she finished her Master of Arts and got a job as a leader at a polytech in Auckland. The work led to a new job and even more studying – this time for her doctorate (PhD).

What are some things Tania did at school?

When Tania went to school, she got certificates that tell people what she's trained to do. Her certificates include a Diploma of Nursing, a Master of Arts and a Doctorate (PhD). Each of her certificates lets Tania do more and bigger jobs.

What certificates do you get at school?

When Tania was studying for her PhD, she decided to research Māori and Pasifika health. But she noticed something: there weren't many books on the subject, information online, or government rules that worked for Māori and Pasifika. So, Tania wrote a paper and she named it *Tangata Hourua.*

Finishing her PhD meant Tania was qualified for many more jobs. She became Head of Nursing Pacific for a polytech in Wellington and loves working in a place where she fits in academically, professionally and culturally. When Tania was young, she didn't know where she fit. She knows now, and she helps other people find where they fit, too.

What is *Tangata Hourua*?

If you don't know your cultural heritage, *Tangata Hourua* can help you figure out who you want to be. It is shaped like a spiral. The lines of the spiral are fixed like DNA. Inside the lines are words that describe who you might be, and you colour in the words that mean something to you.

If you drew a shape and filled it with words that describe you, what shape would it be? What words would you pick?

To find out what DNA is, turn to Parry's story on page 36!

Starship to the Rescue

The story of Starship National Air Ambulance

In Auckland, there is a hospital just for kids. It's called Starship and it has the only intensive care unit dedicated to paediatric patients (kids). Sometimes, kids need to get to there in a hurry so they get flown there on the Starship National Air Ambulance.

The Starship Air Ambulance will pick kids up from hospitals all over New Zealand and the Pacific every day, no matter what time it is. That means some doctors and nurses on the ambulance have to work all night and sleep during the day.

What is your local hospital? Have you ever needed to go? Has someone in your family?

The leader of the Starship National Air Ambulance flight team is a senior nurse named Di Fuller. She thinks that the flight team's job is very tiring, but very rewarding. They travel all over the country helping kids that need them. They are highly trained and very good at their jobs.

The Starship National Air Ambulance makes sure that kids that need to be in intensive care longer than their local hospitals can help them get the care they need.

The Starship Foundation needs to raise a lot of money every year to make sure the Air Ambulance can keep helping kids. Every two days (about every 50 hours), someone needs to be flown to Starship Hospital. In one year, it flew 187 times!

To learn about someone who might have needed help from the Starship Air Ambulance, turn to Hannah's story on page 12!

The Starship National Air Ambulance flies kids from as far away as Invercargill in the South Island, and Kaitaia in the North Island. Can you find Invercargill and Kaitaia on a map?

How long do you think it would take to drive from those cities to Auckland? How much faster do you think the Air Ambulance is?

A Breath of Fresh Air

The story of Jim Bartley

Jim Bartley wanted to be a doctor. He went to medical school to learn about the body and when he graduated, he moved to Nelson to work at the hospital. He was the only doctor working on weekends. He didn't sleep very much because people always needed his help.

He heard that Te Puia Springs needed a doctor so he packed his bags and flew to the North Island. Jim looked after people from Te Puia Springs right up to Te Araroa. He did so many different types of medicine — he delivered babies and he even pulled out people's teeth!

Jim saw lots of Māori patients with problem ears and became interested in ear, nose and throat medicine. He realised that a lot of people with headache and 'sinus pain' also had poor postures and painful necks. He decided to investigate.

He discovered that lots of people had sore muscles, and that's what was making other parts of their bodies hurt. Jim also discovered that lots of people weren't breathing properly! When he taught them how to breathe, properly, they would often get better.

He also found that breathing through your nose helps your brain and influences mood and thinking. The better that you can breathe the better you can focus on daily activities and the better you will sleep.

Jim got so good at helping people get better by breathing that he was asked to work at the Pain Clinic at Auckland Hospital with people who were in a lot of pain. No one else had been able to help them. He did his best and helped as many people as he was able.

To find a health hero who overcame his pain and invented something cool, turn to William's story on page 21!

Health Triumphs

Life can be really hard sometimes, and things can happen to our health that we'd never expect. Read about these seven Kiwi legends who faced very tough times and came out stronger than ever!

1. **Heart-Stopping Moments:** The story of Rob Waddell
2. **The Unstoppable Buttabean:** The story of Dave Letele
3. **Wahine Toa:** The story of Tupou Neiufi
4. **Snow Rider:** The story of Corey Peters
5. **Real Beauty:** The story of Anna Reeve
6. **Kids Can Make a Big Difference:** The story of Eddie Te Hōia (so far)
7. **Weird Symptoms, Rare Disease:** The story of David McPherson

Heart-Stopping Moments

The story of Rob Waddell

Sport was always important to Rob Waddell. One of his proudest moments was when he tried rowing for the first time as a 16 year old. His coach told him if he did well, he'd put him in the First Eight rowing team. He woke up early every day and went to the lake to row, even when it was still dark and cold. Sometimes there was no one else on the lake but him.

Rob rowed so much and got so good he ended up going to the Olympics! Rob represented Aotearoa several times for rowing.

When he left school, Rob noticed something was wrong when he rowed, but he wasn't sure what it was. He wondered if he just didn't believe in himself enough. Maybe he was working too hard on the farm. Or not drinking enough water.

Rob spoke to his uncle who was a doctor. He said that there was something wrong with Rob's heart — something called Atrial Fibrillation. Rob felt so much better knowing the feeling he had when he rowed wasn't just in his head — it was real, and it could be helped by making some changes to his life as well as taking medicine.

Just before the Olympics in Sydney, Australia, Rob's medicine stopped working. His blood wasn't letting the medicine in anymore. He was very worried. His doctors looked after him carefully so that he could still compete.

Rob knew that taking his medicine meant his body would not be working to 100% of its ability. He knew this might be his last time rowing for New Zealand. But still he rowed well and did his best. He did so well that he was the best in the world that day and won a gold medal.

Rob stopped rowing for a while after the Olympics because it was better for his heart. He started sailing instead. He became so good at it that he went on to represent Aotearoa twice in another world competition — the America's Cup.

Rowing was still Rob's passion, and after a few years he decided to give it another go — this time without the medicine. He had to beat another rower in two out of three races to make it to the Olympics and his medicine wouldn't let him do his best. First he raced and won. Then he raced and lost. And during the final race, his heart felt strange, like he was rowing through jelly. He lost that race.

New Zealand didn't know about his heart. People thought Rob had just given up. But Rob didn't care what people thought — he was proud of himself. Rob said, 'Life is bigger than one race, it's about who you are as a person . . . you do the best you can.'

Rob didn't give up on going back to the Olympics. He and a friend decided to row together and they went to the Olympics as a team. They came fourth in their race and did New Zealand proud.

A year after that race, Rob couldn't even walk up stairs without his heart playing up and he decided to have surgery. His heart is much better now and he doesn't need medicine anymore. Sometimes, when Rob doesn't get enough sleep or works too much, his heart skips a beat. This reminds him to look after himself better.

To find the story of a doctor who wants you to look after yourself as much as Rob, turn to Jim's story on page 52!

The Unstoppable Buttabean

The story of Dave Letele

Dave Letele thinks of his life like a rollercoaster. When he was born, the rollercoaster was close to the ground, then as he got older it climbed and climbed. When he became an adult, the rollercoaster reached the top before speeding back down to the ground. Dave's rollercoaster is climbing back to the top again, slowly and carefully. And this time he's got a lot of people on the rollercoaster supporting him.

When he was young, Dave's life was very hard. His dad did a lot of dangerous things and wasn't around much. Every day was a struggle, and Dave knew that he didn't want life to be a struggle when he was an adult.

He worked hard in school, and when he grew up he travelled to Australia to study and play Rugby League. He was good at league and made a lot of money which he used to buy supermarkets, becoming a league-playing businessman. His rollercoaster was at the top.

One day, Dave lost everything and had to move home to Auckland to live with his sister. He felt broken. Every day was a struggle, and he weighed 210kg.

One day, he struggled his way out of bed and went for a walk up Maungakiekie | One Tree Hill. He thought to himself, 'This is one steep hill. Why did I choose this place to start?' But he realised everyone needs to start somewhere.

Dave started boxing with the help of his friend and became known as the Brown Buttabean. His job was to pretend to be the bad guy. Lots of people thought that meant Dave was a bad guy in real life and people bullied him online.

Then one day, instead of being mean to him, someone asked what his secret was – how was he losing so much weight? He had lost about 100kg at this point. Dave said that there's no secret. Eat healthy, drink water and go for a walk. He started an online group for people who wanted to talk to him as Dave, rather than being mean to the Brown Buttabean.

One by one he started helping people exercise. And then he started helping a lot of people at a time by running boot camps. During the COVID-19 pandemic, people had a lot more time to cook healthy and exercise, but many people were struggling to access food. Again, Dave stepped in to help. He started a food-share service in South Auckland. Slowly but surely, Dave's rollercoaster was going uphill again, with everyone he was helping on board, too.

When Dave was playing league, he was taught all about food and how to eat to get the best out of his body. The online group he started asked a lot of questions about how to eat healthy. Dave taught them what he knew.

Since the COVID-19 lockdowns ended, everyone has become busy again. People don't have as much time to look after themselves; to cook healthy food and exercise. Dave said he's seen too many people choose to eat what is fast and easy because they don't have time to cook, and often this can be unhealthy.

Dave wants you to remember to look after yourself. He wants you to learn about food, go for walks, and remember to be nice to people online. He wants you to try new things, and if they don't go well then you can learn from your failures. Never be afraid of trying.

To learn about someone who teaches kids about healthy food, turn to Catherine's story on page 44!

Wahine Toa

The story of Tupou Neiufi

When Tupou Neiufi was two years old, something awful happened. She ran out of her front yard into the street and got hit by a car. It wasn't anyone's fault. It was just an accident.

The car that hit Tupou hurt her brain. She has left-side hemiplegia, which means the left side of her body is smaller and weaker than the right side. It also means that her brain works a bit more slowly to understand things. Sometimes Tupou slurs her words.

When she was young, she had help working her muscles to make her stronger. She also had help learning how to read, and how to speak clearly. Our brains need just as much exercise as our muscles.

Tupou spent ages in hospital. She was looked after every day by doctors and nurses. Tupou had just learnt to walk, but they didn't think she would ever be able to walk again.

Every day, Tupou's mum and dad helped her sit up in her hospital bed. She had pillows at her back and along her sides to hold her up. Every day, she tried harder and harder until one day she could sit up all by herself. Then it was time to try and stand up. Once she could stand, it was time to learn how to walk again. She worked on it every day until she could walk again. Tupou nailed it!

When Tupou was seven, she started playing netball. She thought she was pretty good! But one day her mum stopped taking her her to netball because she was worried about Tupou getting hurt. Sometimes she couldn't catch the ball, and it hurt when it hit her hands. Her mum started looking for a more gentle sport.

Someone said Tupou should try swimming. Her mum and dad were worried — water safety is really important in Aotearoa, and we all know not to go into the deep end of the pool without an adult. Tupou started swimming and she had to use her left side to make sure she didn't sink. Her left side got stronger and stronger, and Tupou got faster and faster.

When she was young, Tupou's favourite thing about swimming was how nice the water felt when it was a hot day. Have you ever got into a pool when you were hot and felt the water cool you down?

Tupou's second favourite thing about swimming was making new friends.

Tupou got so fast that someone said she could compete at the Paralympics. The best of the best athletes with disabilities get to go to the Paralympics. She started training hard, swimming every morning before school, and when the bell rang at 3pm, she was back in the pool. Every day, her mum drove her and her sisters from Ōtāhuhu to Pakuranga to get to the pool.

She did okay at her first Paralympic Games but didn't win any medals. When she went to the Paralympics for the second time, everyone thought she would come third. She had her headphones on, and listening to Rihanna was getting her pumped for the race. When Tupou walked out to the pool, people were taking her photo and the whole world was watching. She tried to look cool but when she got to the pool she realised — this was real. She began to panic and get shaky. But she remembered to breathe to calm herself down.

During the race, Tupou could see everyone's arms spinning through the water. She said to herself, 'It's either them or me'. She swam her hardest and touched the wall to finish the race. One of her teammates was screaming her head off when Tupou touched the wall. She thought she must have won a medal. She didn't know she had won a gold until she took off her goggles. When she realised, all her feelings rushed up and she almost cried.

Every day, Tupou is grateful for her parents and sisters. They supported her dreams. and helped her win her medals. These days Tupou supports others. She gives talks on mental health and mentors other Polynesian kids who are playing sports. She knows they can be great and succeed, because she was once just like them.

Tupou was only 15 when she first swam for New Zealand at the Paralympics! At 19 she won a gold medal in the 100m backstroke S8.

She has silver and bronze medals, too. She won them at world championships and the Commonwealth Games.

To learn about another heath hero who couldn't have done it without their family, turn to Colin's story on page 24!

Snow Rider

The story of Corey Peters

When Corey Peters was little, his friends said they wanted to be policemen or firemen, but he wasn't sure he wanted to be either of those. Or anything else his friends said they wanted to be as they got older. Corey liked sports. He played rugby and cricket, he skateboarded and tried surfing. Corey liked sports a lot, but he didn't think he could make a career out of it.

The older he got the more he thought about being a builder — he had done woodworking at school and thought it could be a cool job. When he left school, he built things out of wood to go on really big boats.

Corey still loved sports and kept trying new ones. His brother started doing motocross and Corey thought he would try it, too. They went with their dad to the track and Corey got on his bike to race.

He was going really fast when he went over a jump and landed badly. His back was hurt, and his legs felt like water balloons. He couldn't feel them properly or sit up. It was very scary.

Corey was in hospital for months and months. He had to move from New Plymouth to Christchurch to see the best doctors for his spine. He was angry and frustrated and his mental health was not good.

What happened to Corey's back?

Your back has a spine — bones that go from your head to your bum called vertebrae. The bones all stack on top of each other like blocks, and they all have a hole in them for the spinal cord to run down from your brain. The bones protect the spinal cord and keep it safe. We need our spinal cord to work properly so parts of our bodies like our legs can work. When Corey landed funny, he fractured (broke or cracked) his vertebrae and damaged his spinal cord at the same time.

The doctor told Corey he might never walk again but Corey decided he would prove the doctor wrong. He listened to everyone that was working together to help him: the doctors, nurses and physiotherapists, and it took years to get his body working again!

Corey can feel a lot of his legs now, but he doesn't really have any muscles in the back of them, including his bum and calf muscles. This means that while he can walk with crutches, he spends a lot of time in his wheelchair.

He was finally able to move home to New Plymouth, where he met a new friend named Ian. Ian had hurt his back, too, and liked sports as much as Corey. He told Corey about all the wheelchair-accessible sports he had tried, and one of them was skiing with something called a Sit Ski. Corey bought one, and he and Ian went skiing on Mount Ruapehu.

Corey loved skiing! He used the skills he had learnt from surfing and motocross, and he got really good at it. Sit Skiing gave Corey a new purpose; something to work towards. He went on a skiing holiday to Wānaka, and some experts saw how good he was. They said he should go and train in America where he could get even better.

Corey followed their advice and got so good he was asked to ski for New Zealand at the Paralympics! He had watched other skiers and been inspired by them. Now he was skiing with them! He won a silver medal at his first Paralympic Games. He felt amazing standing up on the podium next to the winners of the gold and bronze medals. Corey went to two more Paralympic Games and won gold and bronze medals — he now has the whole set!

To learn about another health hero who went to America to achieve their dream, turn to Ehsan's story on page 32!

After he hurt his back, Corey had to work hard on his body, and he had to work hard at skiing, too. Every day he tried to be better than yesterday. He didn't care if he was better than someone else — he only cared that he was better than he was the day before. It was important to Corey that he always had fun doing what he loved, and always tried his hardest.

What do you work hard at? Do you try to do your best at it every day?

Real Beauty

The story of Anna Reeve

When Anna Reeve was a kid, her dad was a pilot who got to travel all over the world. Sometimes Anna, her mum and her brother would get join him! When he wasn't flying, her dad liked to go sailing, so they spent a lot of time on the ocean. Anna's favourite spot to go sailing in New Zealand is the Bay of Islands, Taitokerau | Northland.

Anna was seven when her mum thought she was cutting pieces of her hair off like she did to her dolls. Then she spotted something weird happening to one of Anna's eyebrows — it looked patchy, like the hair was coming out. Some of the kids in Anna's class thought she looked weird. One of the girls said Anna looked like her grandad because she only had little bits of hair. The kids bullied Anna because she didn't look like everyone else.

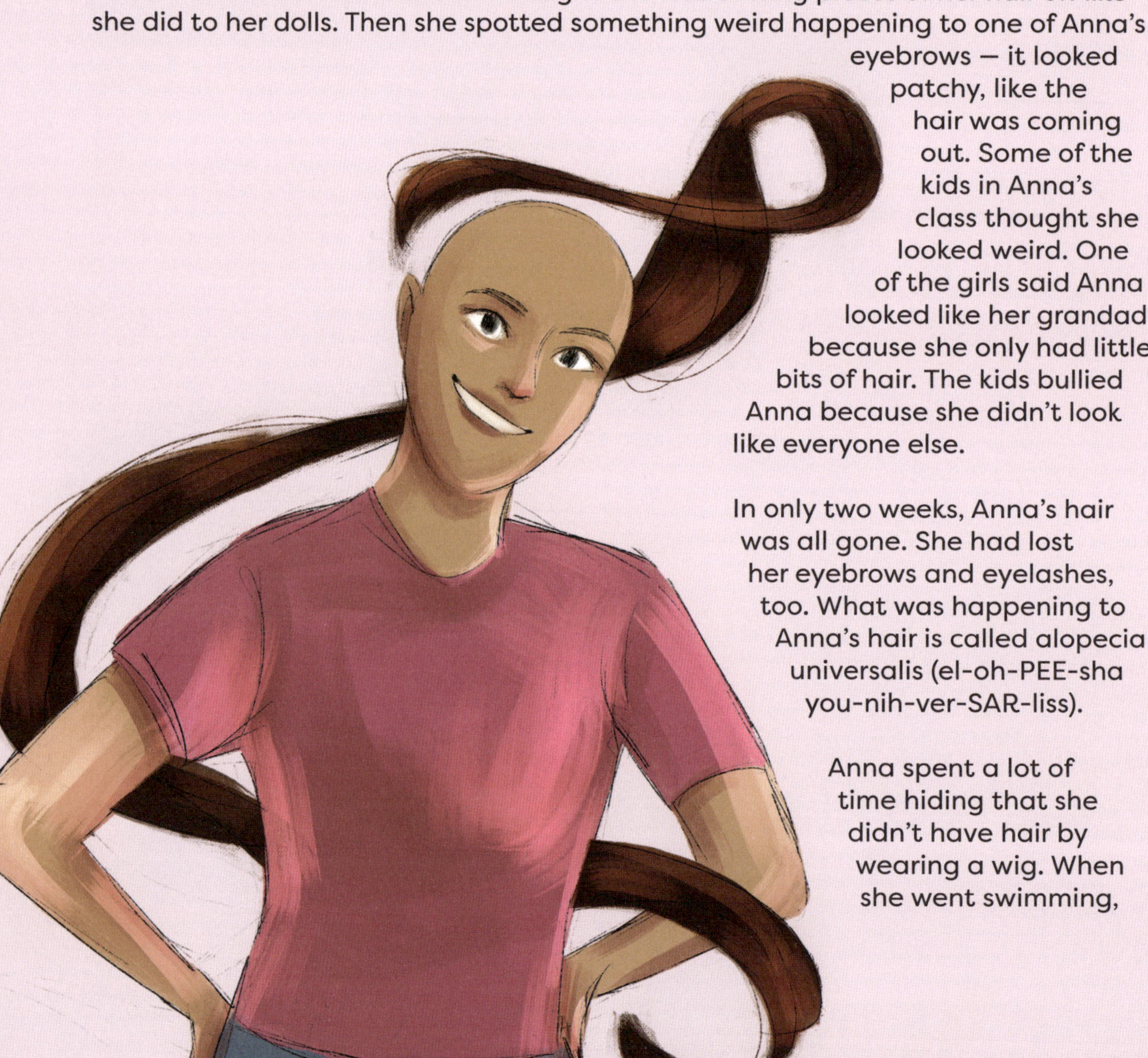

In only two weeks, Anna's hair was all gone. She had lost her eyebrows and eyelashes, too. What was happening to Anna's hair is called alopecia universalis (el-oh-PEE-sha you-nih-ver-SAR-liss).

Anna spent a lot of time hiding that she didn't have hair by wearing a wig. When she went swimming,

Anna would put a swimming cap on so people couldn't see her baldness. When she was in town, she wore a hat. Anna didn't want her mum to tell anyone at school that she had alopecia.

At a school camp, everyone found out Anna was bald when she was on a waterslide and her wig fell off. She wanted to leave camp, but her mum encouraged her to stay. They explained to everyone that Anna had a medical condition that made her lose her hair.

What is Alopecia Universalis?

Your body has something called an immune system. The immune system is supposed to fight germs and diseases, but sometimes it decides to fight something your body is supposed to have. When your immune system fights your hair follicles, it makes the hair fall out. That's called alopecia. Alopecia Universalis is when hair falls out on your whole body.

When Anna grew up, someone said she could be a model. She decided to try it and was scared when she took her wig off for her first photoshoot. She thought people might not like the photos, and that they might want her to wear her wig all the time.

Everyone loved Anna as she was, and her photos were printed in magazines. Sometimes she wore a wig and sometimes she didn't. Modelling helped Anna accept and be proud of what she looks like.

When she was a kid, Anna didn't know anyone who looked like her. She was scared to show the world who she was. Now, Anna can be herself every day — some days she's bald, and some days she wears one of her wigs. But every day, Anna knows that she's amazing, strong and honest with the world about who she is.

How do we treat people who look different to us?

We should treat people the way we want to be treated. Would you like it if someone was mean to you?

Or would you like to be a good friend who is kind to people?

To learn about another amazing and strong woman turn to Tupou's story on page 58!

Kids Can Make a Big Difference

The story of Eddie Te Hōia (so far)

'Ko Taranaki te maunga
Ko Waitara te awa
Ko Tokomaru te waka
Ko Ngāti Mutunga te iwi
Nō Wharekauri ahau
Ko Eddie Te Hōia tōku ingoa'

Eddie Te Hōia is a kid. He has a family, he goes to school, he has friends. Eddie also has Type 1 diabetes. He was diagnosed when he was only six years old, and it was very scary. He didn't know why he was in hospital, and he didn't know why he was getting injections. It wasn't his first time in hospital though, so Eddie knew how to make friends with other kids while he was there.

Eddie's hospital friends were there for all sorts of reasons. The doctors, nurses and other hospital staff looked after them well, but the hospital was a bit run down. Eddie decided he wanted to help by raising as much money as he could to donate to the hospital.

When Eddie was four, he raised $15,000 for Wellington Hospital! He walked around Wellington raising money, and asked people to donate for his birthday instead of getting him presents. When he reached $15,000, he donated all the money to the hospital.

Eddie got to go home from the hospital, but his life was different from other kids. Having Type 1 diabetes meant Eddie needed to prick his fingers all the time with a needle to see how much sugar was in his blood. His fingers got really sore, and sometimes they got infected with germs, too. If Eddie's blood sugar wasn't at the right level it often meant he needed to have an injection. That meant two needles! Often, Eddie had to have ten injections a day. He was super brave.

One of Eddie's doctors tried out a cool medical device on Eddie's arm — a Continuous Glucose Monitor, or CGM. The monitor continuously checked the amount of sugar in Eddie's blood, so he didn't have to prick his fingers anymore!

Well . . . he didn't have to prick them for two weeks. That's how long a CGM lasts before it needs replacing. They are really expensive, so not everyone who needs them can afford them. Eddie thought this wasn't fair, and it made him sad. Why couldn't everyone with Type 1 diabetes in Aotearoa have one?

Eddie came up with a plan. He was going to write to politicians and the media to get on TV and make his voice heard. Eddie became the youngest person to speak at parliament, which is also known as the Beehive.

He made a special trip to the Beehive to listen to the budget being announced hoping that CGMs would be funded in the new health budget. But they weren't. So, Eddie kept trying. He continued writing to politicians and raising awareness where he could. He kept talking to everyone he could. And eventually, in October 2024, CGMs got funded for everyone in New Zealand that needs them.

Eddie doesn't have to prick his fingers anymore. Now, every two weeks he swaps which arm has the CGM on it. His fingers don't hurt anymore, and he can sleep through the night.

His mum says she's so proud of him. His whānau is proud, his ancestors are proud, and his community are proud. He didn't give up and he changed the lives of thousands of New Zealanders.

Eddie's tips on how to be a good friend to someone with Type 1 diabetes:

- **Don't always ask about it — your friends like to talk about a lot of things, not just diabetes.**
- **Be there for your friend if they want to talk.**
- **Support them if they need help.**
- **Stand up for them if someone tries to bully them.**

To learn about other cool medical technology, turn to the story about Fisher & Paykel Healthcare on page 30!

Weird Symptoms, Rare Disease

The story of David McPherson

When David McPherson was born, he had three much older siblings. His older brother was 20, and his sisters were 13 and 14. It was almost like he had three mums because his sisters looked after him a lot while their mum worked. David and his family all lived in Marton.

When he was two years old, his mum noticed strange bumps on his tongue and took him to the doctor. The doctor said he might have an infection, but David had some hidden symptoms that the doctor couldn't see. After a few days of treatment, David's mum decided to take him back to the doctor because she'd noticed his hands and feet were peeling, and his eyes were red and swollen. He was also sleeping a lot — which was weird for David, who hadn't slept through the night in the two years since he'd been born.

David's usual doctor was away so they saw a different doctor this time. He had moved to New Zealand from another country and had seen David's symptoms a lot at home. The doctor said to David's mum, 'I don't want to worry you, but you need to take him to Palmerston North Hospital right now.' She asked what was wrong and he said that he thought it was Kawasaki disease.

What is Kawasaki disease?

It's a rare illness that children can get. Most children who get the disease are five years old or younger. It makes blood vessels and sometimes the heart swell up, and there is a risk of coronary aneurysms. The blood vessels and heart can be damaged and sometimes people can die.

No one knows what causes it, but it isn't contagious so can't be passed from person to person.

There are quite a few symptoms and can include a rash, a red tongue, and swollen and peeling hands and feet.

When they got to the hospital, David was admitted to the children's ward right away. They did all the normal tests, and then it was time for his blood test. David was wrapped up in a hospital sheet with just his arm sticking out. Although his mum was holding him, David was terrified and wouldn't hold still. She needed help from four more people to hold him still so they could take his blood.

Even though David was very sick, he had the zoomies at the hospital and ran around the ward in circles. The nurses couldn't believe how much energy he had. What David and his family didn't know, was that he had ADHD, which was winning against the Kawasaki disease.

David had to have X-rays, and a heart scan. But his ADHD-fuelled zoomies meant the radiologist couldn't get David to sit still long enough. They said he would have to be transferred to Whanganui Hospital as there was someone from Green Lane Hospital in Auckland who could do the heart scans.

In Whanganui, the hospital staff tried to sedate David so he'd be calm and quiet for his scans, which didn't work, so they kept giving him more and more sedation. They were astounded that he was still able to run around the ward. His mum took him for a drive to get a pie, then back to the hospital when he fell asleep. Finally he was able to have his heart scan.

David was given blood thinners for six months to make sure his heart and blood vessels wouldn't get damaged. One day, his oldest sister took him to Vinegar Hill for a swim in the river. Their mum had told her not to take his shoes off, but his sister did anyway. David cut his foot on glass in the river and it wouldn't stop bleeding.

She rang their mum in a panic and they drove back to Marton to pick up their mum before heading to the emergency doctor in Palmerston North. The nurse who saw them glued David's foot back together but it didn't hold and his foot split back open, and got infected. It got glued together again, and this time it held. David still has a jagged scar on his foot to this day.

David is now 21 years old. He doesn't remember much about having Kawasaki disease because he was so young. He remembers being scared and in a lot of pain. His mum remembers everything — including that when he was running around the hospital, he was so much faster than her.

To learn about a health hero who can do x-rays, turn to Anthony's story on page 28!

Advice from our Health Heroes

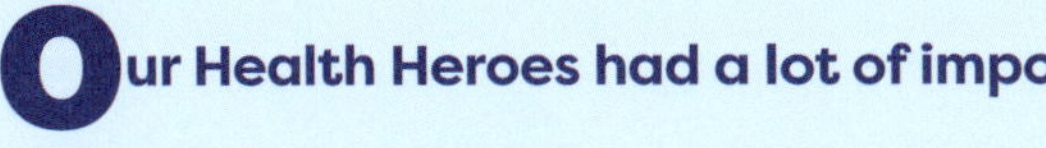

Our Health Heroes had a lot of important things to share with you.

Sir Ashley Bloomfield
'I probably wasn't the world's best waiter, but one of the things that it taught me, and I have passed this on to my children, is if you want to go places in life, work hard and be nice to people.'

Corey Peters
'Something I have learnt through this accident is that everyone has to have goals in life in order to have a real purpose. Each day you must have something to work towards.'

Tania Mullane
'We need progress, not perfection. Perfection is almost unobtainable. If you're going to go for perfection, then you're going to sit there all day. If we go for progress, we are moving forward.'

Parry Guilford
'Find what you're into and then chase it with all of your might.'

Dave Letele
'Everyone is destined for greatness . . . the good life belongs to us all. You just have to start, keep going and never let excuses get in your way.'

Rob Waddell
'It's easy to do things when the sun is shining, but when it's raining and cold . . . that's when it really matters and that's when you need to do your best.'

Anthony Butler
'I wish I was better at realising when I have made a mistake. But we all make mistakes. It's normal.'

Leanne Te Karu
'The greatest untapped resource . . . is ourselves.'

Credits

Nurse Maude
Caring for the community since 1896
Providing Homecare, District Nursing, Specialty Clinics, School Based Nursing, a Care Home and Hospice Palliative Care Services

Peter Button QBE QGM
(9 October 1929–20 November 1987)
Pioneering Rescue Helicopter Pilot
Founder, Capital Helicopters
Co-founder, Life Flight Trust
Officer of the Order of the British Empire (1982)
Recipient, Queen's Gallantry Medal (1987)
Wellington, New Zealand

Hannah Butler
Daughter of Reverend John Gare and Hannah Butler
Child of the Church Missionary Society

George Hamlin
Son of James and Elizabeth Hamlin
Child of the Church Missionary Society

Jean Sandel
(26 December 1916–4 November 1974)
MBChB
Director of Surgery, New Plymouth Hospital
Fellow of the Royal College of Surgeons and Royal Australasian College of Surgeons

Dr Elizabeth Gunn MBE
(23 May 1879–26 October 1963)
Public health advocate
Captain, New Zealand Medical Corps
Founder, Children's Health Camp movement

Dr Peter Snow
(11 November 1934–28 February 2006)
New Zealand General Practitioner
Served the community of Tapanui for over 30 years
Identified 'Tapanui flu' (chronic fatigue syndrome) in 1984
President, Royal New Zealand College of General Practitioners (1998–1999)
Member, Otago Hospital Board and Otago District Health Board (15 years)

Sir Ashley Bloomfield KNZM
MBChB, MPH, FNZCPHM
Former Director-General of Health
Professor, School of Public Health, University of Auckland | Waipapa Taumata Rau

Catherine Bell
New Zealand culinary entrepreneur
Founder of Epicurean Workshop and Epicure Trading
Advocate for sustainable dining and ethical sourcing
Founder of Garden to Table initiative supporting children's food education
Board, Chair Garden to Table Charitable Trust
Author of three cookbooks

Leanne Te Karu
Muaūpoko/Whanganui Ngāti Rangi, Ngāti Kurawhatia, Ngāti Patutokotoko
DipPharm, PGCertHerbalMeds, PGDipClinPharm, MHSc(Hons), PGCert(Prescribing), PhD(Auckland)

Dr Tania Mullane
New Zealand Nursing Educator & Health Leader
Head of Nursing Pacific at Whitireia | Te Pūkenga
Advocate for Pacific and Māori health equity
Pioneer in indigenising nursing education in New Zealand
Leader in Pacific Nursing workforce development
Researcher in improving health outcomes for Māori and Pacific communities
Co-author on Indigenous research and health frameworks

Starship Foundation
Charity partner of Aotearoa's national children's hospital, Starship
Fundraising organisation, supporting Aotearoa's sick and injured children

Dr Jim Bartley
MBChB, FRACS
Retired Consultant Otolaryngologist, Te Whatu Ora
Honorary Associate Professor of Surgery, University of Auckland | Waipapa Taumata Rau
Expert in Sleep and Breathing Disorder

William Pike
Proud dad
Adventurer
Founder of the William Pike Challenge
Inspirational speaker
Inventor of PRO ARMOUR®

Colin Murdoch ONZM
(6 February 1929–4 May 2008)
Pharmacist
Inventor
Founder of Paxarms Limited
Royal Humane Society Medal winner

Lorraine Parthemore
Registered Nurse
Practice Manager/RN at Coastal Orthopaedics, New Plymouth, New Zealand
Inventor of the Parthemore Pulley, used in spinal surgery

Anthony Butler
MBChB, PhD, GradDipSc, FRANZCR
Professor of Radiology, University of Otago | Ōtākou Whakaihu Waka
Founder and Chief Medical Officer, MARS Bioimaging
Consultant Radiologist, Te Whatu Ora

Fisher & Paykel Healthcare
A leading designer, manufacturer and marketer of products and systems for use in acute and chronic respiratory care, surgery and the treatment of obstructive sleep apnoea

Ehsan Vaghefi
PhD (Bioengineering and Biomedical Engineering)
CEO and co-founder, Toku Eyes

Sir Graham Liggins
(24 June 1926–24 August 2010)
CBE, FRS, FRSNZ
Professor at the University of Auckland | Waipapa Taumata Rau
Eponym of the Liggins Institute

Parry Guilford
BSc, MSc
Professor of Cancer Genetics, University of Otago | Ōtākou Whakaihu Waka
Director, Centre for Translational Cancer Research
Co-Founder, Pacific Edge Ltd

Sid Yarrow
(1923–23 May 2011)
Royal Air Force electronics engineer
Inventor and innovator
First perfusionist in New Zealand
Life Member of the Australia and New Zealand College of Perfusionists
Eponym of the Sid Yarrow Award, founded in 1993

Rob Waddell ONZM
Gold medal-winning Olympic and World Championship rower
America's Cup yachtsman
Multi-Halberg Award winner
Lonsdale Cup winner

Dave Letele
Retired rugby league player and professional boxer
Motivational speaker
Community leader
Founder of Brown Buttabean Motivation
Pacific People's Award special honour award winner
Kiwibank New Zealand Local Hero of the Year 2022

Tupou Neiufi
Tongan-New Zealand Paralympic, Commonwealth, and World Para swimmer
Gold, silver and bronze medallist
Pacific Health and Wellbeing Award winner
Tongan Youth Excellence Award winner

Corey Peters MNZM
Alpine skier
Paralympic gold, silver and bronze medallist
Multi-award-winning athlete
Para Athlete of the Year 2022

Anna Reeve
Proud mum
New Zealand Model, Influencer, and alopecia Advocate
Co-founder of Pals, a ready-to-drink beverage brand
Co-winner of 'The Traitors NZ' Season 1

Eddie Te Hōia
Big brother
Proud Moriori and Māori
Type 1 diabetes advocate
Vaccination champion

David McPherson
Ngāti Porou
Autistic and ADHD
Aspiring voice actor

Thanks to the following organisations and individuals for use of their images to inspire So-Young;
Unknown [circa 1960], Sid Yarrow and Nurse Shona Budd demonstrates the Melrose heart-lung machine, 06/071/003, Walsh Memorial Library Museum of Transport & Technology (MOTAT)
William Pike, Avoca Valley, Southern Alps. (MITCH THORN)
Rob Waddell, Sydney 2000 (PHOTO SPORT)
South Canterbury Museum #2022/186.6632. Inventor and former chemist Colin Murdoch, pictured with two of his inventions: a disposable hypodermic syringe and a telescopic rifle sight, circa 1991.

Thanks to the following people and organisation for the interviews and information that inspired Caitlin and Bex; Tania Mullane, Rob Waddell, William Pike, Sir Ashley Bloomfield, Marilyn Murdoch, Leanne Te Karu, Catherine Bell, Dave Letele, Anthony Butler, Fisher & Paykel Healthcare, Jackie Liggins, MOTAT, the Life Flight Trust, Eshan Vaghefi, Parry Guilford, James Bartley, Corey Peters, Tupou Neiufi, Anna Reeve, Eddie Te Hōia and his mum Emily, Lorraine Parthemore, the Nurse Maude Foundation, the Starship Foundation, Adrian Snow, and David McPherson and his mum, Ali.

Published in 2026 by David Bateman Ltd,
Unit 2/5 Workspace Drive, Hobsonville,
Auckland 0618, New Zealand
www.batemanbooks.co.nz
ISBN: 978-1-77689-168-9

A catalogue record for this book is available from the National Library of New Zealand.

Printed in China by Toppan Leefung Printing Ltd